DISSOLVE to: L.A.

RAMBO
Do we get to win this time?

TRAUTMAN
This time it's up to you.

Rambo: First Blood Part II

OTHER BOOKS FROM THE EMMA PRESS

POETRY ANTHOLOGIES

Homesickness and Exile: Poems about Longing and Belonging
Best Friends Forever: Poems on Female Friendship
Campaign in Poetry
The Emma Press Anthology of Dance
Slow Things: Poems about Slow Things
The Emma Press Anthology of Age
Mildly Erotic Verse
Urban Myths and Legends (June '16)

POETRY ANTHOLOGIES FOR CHILDREN

Falling Out of the Sky: Poems about Myths and Monsters

THE EMMA PRESS PICKS

The Emmores, by Richard O'Brien
The Held and the Lost, by Kristen Roberts
Captain Love and the Five Joaquins, by John Clegg
Malkin, by Camille Ralphs

POETRY PAMPHLETS

Oils, by Stephen Sexton
Myrtle, by Ruth Wiggins
If I Lay on my Back I Saw Nothing but Naked Women,
by Jacqueline Saphra and Mark Andrew Webber
True Tales of the Countryside, by Deborah Alma
AWOL, by John Fuller and Andrew Wynn Owen
Goose Fair Night, by Kathy Pimlott
Mackerel Salad, by Ben Rogers (May '16)
Trouble, by Alison Winch (May '16)

DISSOLVE to: L.A.

Action movie poems by James Trevelyan
Illustrations by Emma Wright

THE EMMA PRESS

for my sister, Anna

THE EMMA PRESS

First published in Great Britain in 2016
by the Emma Press Ltd

Poems copyright © James Trevelyan 2016
Illustrations copyright © Emma Wright 2016

All rights reserved.

The right of James Trevelyan to be identified as the
author of this work has been asserted by him in accordance
with the Copyright, Designs and Patents Act 1988.

ISBN 978-1-910139-37-0

A CIP catalogue record of this book
is available from the British Library.

Printed and bound in Great Britain
by Letterworks Ltd, Reading.

theemmapress.com
queries@theemmapress.com

CONTENTS

LLOYD	1
HAWKINS	3
BENNY	7
TIMMY	8
ADMIRAL CHUCK FARRELL	9
DONALD GENNARO	11
COUGAR	14
GIRL	17
TONY	18
MIKEY TANDINO	20
GARLAND GREENE	22
HELEN	25
Notes	27
Acknowledgements	29
About the poet and illustrator	29
About the Emma Press	30

LLOYD

DISSOLVE to: L.A. – '95, PRESENT DAY

They gave me a name
and does that not give me life?
More at least than UNIFORMED COP,
NIGHT NURSE or FIRST JOCK,

who may have had more to say
but can't claim to an existence
beyond their scene. I suppose
they forgot me, but I'll not

forget the night a naked
colossus walked into my bar, eyes
steely with intent. A Titan:
Atlas, having shaken the burden

at this Western edge of the earth,
eclipsed now by a different purpose
and fearing no consequences. You'll
remember my 10-GAUGE WINCHESTER

LEVER-ACTION SHOTGUN could reload
by the swing of one strong arm,
and my sunglasses so dark
they'd protect your eyes from the white

light of Judgment Day. But you may fail
to recall – before he took
these from me – that I spoke
to this creature like a brother,

its first lesson in humanity: *I can't
let you take the man's wheels, son.*
He drove off. I sold, moved
up-state, never replaced my gun.

HAWKINS

*Hawkins follows, his mouth open, breathing
deeply, exhausted, the radio a 60 pound demon.*

– The Thomas Brothers

Don't call me kid. I might
not smoke cigars the size
of a Colt .45, but I am more
than the skid of a jungle
scorpion on your sole.

I should've known I was first to go
when I saw my pack:
the maps, the field phone,

with a pair of specs
reaching almost
to my mouth – gold rims
and glass shimmering –
my camo paint redundant.

Where's my history? *Back in '72*
I was still in school and carry with me
only overheard jokes

on the size of a fictional
girlfriend's sexual organs.
I don't know

what you must think of me,
honestly, I wouldn't

normally resort to smut,
but I was trying to fit in with guys
who chewed tobacco; men

who *ain't got time to bleed.*
I suppose I was freed
as that monster cut through
my chest and strung me up
a ceiba tree. That moment

was more
than a plot device, it was
my purpose in life:

only after I met death,
face-to-face, did those
left alive realise
it is we
who are being chased.

BENNY

An illegal-arms bust and I'm riddled
with bullets, and it can't matter –
amid this hot fug of Assam and Jasmine,
the teashop clamour of budgerigars –
that I'm a good guy, just that tomorrow
there'll be one less cop for them to buy.

Laid out now on a floor that shimmers
and swills like the deck of the whaling ship
I worked that young winter, blood
and water collecting at my sides, salt
climbing in each breath, I clutch
as I did then for a reason

and greet only blubber and meat.
I've a sad feeling – in the absence
of anything real – someone will avenge me,
or try. Rising towards the vaulted ceiling,
birds and imperial beams I'm left to wonder
how they ever hung these cages so high.

TIMMY

rebecca you got my ass tanned so many times with your climbing and crawling your sticky fingers your bawling and lying how youd tell dad I hit you when it was just a game rebecca im gonna call you by your name even if you dont like it even if mum says I should love my sister and call you what you choose i know they just agree to call you newt because theyre happy youve something that distracts you and they hate our lives on Acheron and are sick to death of the fake air and pounding rain that and your bugeyes and cold blood i bet you dont remember a star that warms you up mum says newts could regrow a leg if they got it torn off and sometimes i think ill try on you dad told me he loved you more when he was drunk and manic from loneliness you were always daddys girl even when that monster took his mouth and planted itself in the dark inside it was your name that flaked his lips newt it was your shape that burst from his heart

ADMIRAL CHUCK FARRELL

"Xenia... I can't breathe!"

You had me at your name and innuendo, your made-up cod-Russian sweet nothings, your fatal frame and martini twist; might have known a Ferrari-toting Soviet pilot might come with added spice, but the biting and the growling in the hotel bed sure came as a surprise.

I wonder where you learnt those moves, whose eyes you first saw bulging as their ribs caved in, whose blood could not return to flood their brain with time enough to spare. Onatopp, I would share more than my life, suit and security card to die between your thighs again.

DONALD GENNARO

"When you gotta go, you gotta go."
– DR IAN MALCOLM

Elvis you remember – rhythmic hips,
All-American drawl – how he first broke hearts
in the dancehall, then on a tiled floor,

propped by the cistern, arteries
of an eighty-year-old.
So you can't have forgotten my own demise,

seized from the john by the hot bite
of Tyrannosaur jaws: the first human
to witness the inside

of a bastard dinosaur's mouth,
feel its gravel lick and slick manoeuvring
of teeth; to understand how it is

to be lifted from your seat
twenty feet by a living creation.
Why not honour my uniqueness

from island jungle to Tokyo.
Make me a wiki page. Put me in
a Hall of Fame with The King and the others.

Celebrate my name, Gennaro,
but let Donald be enough to signify.
Believe in my existence beyond the grave

and know in a Midwest town
you've never been to sit reams
of late-twenties impersonators

in A CITY MAN'S IDEA OF HIKING CLOTHES
and the same HUNDRED DOLLAR HAIRCUT,
dreaming of Vegas shows and saving up

for theme park commodes. One
has papier-mâchéd a six-foot open mouth,
built a garden toilet, set the walls and door

to collapse at the pull of a cord
and will invite his friends this Thanksgiving
morning, when his mother will push go

on the sound effects and drop fate from an upstairs
window, encourage the meagre crowd
to search the bushes for her son's remains.

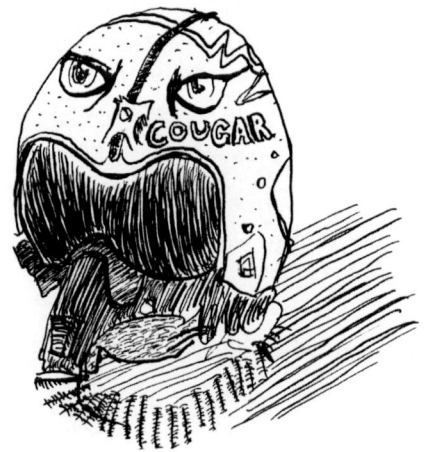

COUGAR

Guide me in, Maverick,
you live your life in the skies and between your legs,
and I've seen you rouse a bar full of pilots and blondes
into singing your song. You're a one-off, Maverick,
like your father was, and if I manage to stay
on your wing I know you'll take me all the way in.

Guide me in, Iceman,
slide me on a frozen jet stream,
throw this catamount down the mountain,
let me tumble in your avalanche and come to
rest on the steep rock of your face,
sleep curled in its cave for a cool decade.

Guide me in, Jester,
call me floozie, milf, molester;
call me cradle-snatcher, spring-semester.
Jester, *meow* at my comebacks,
call me pussycat in front of the guys. Call my name,
Jester, look me in the eyes, and I'll call yours.

Guide me in, Goose,
fly me in formation, pull the ejectors,
be my mate. You were truly hatched
of a golden egg. Teach us the ways
of monogamy and treat me to a rest
in the downy feather of your pit.

Guide me in, Hollywood,
with your turbo complexion
and hair metal. I'll follow the shine
of your teeth and behind,
Hollywood, your rudderless bronze
chassis is catnip to me.

Guide me in, Wolfman,
and I'll cling to your roar, ride
on your back like an oxpecker, because
I've seen your clod paws thwack
a volleyball hard enough to know
I lack every inch of you.

Guide me in, Sundown,
you always had my number and know
I'm no growler, no alleycat. That last flight
you reached inside my squinting eyes, bounced
around the cockpit, and brought me down,
belly up, engines purring.

GIRL

Why always Christmas time;
always *Jingle Bell Rock;*
the threat of snow.

Why always the slow pan across the cityscape;
open window, billowing drapes;
always the top floor.

Why always the potential heroine;
the pretty girl in a silk slip;
breast and nipple carefully displayed.

Why always alone, writhing in sleep, wakefulness, ecstasy;
coke over the coffee-table;
always a dodgy batch.

Why always making a grab for fame;
the good girl fallen;
the prominent dad downtown.

Why always naked, wasted;
testing the strength of the balcony fence;
always weightless and hilarious.

Why a car bonnet that breaks the fall;
the shirt always open, not a hair out of place,
like Ophelia or a centrefold.

TONY

> *"We do it the hard way!* [He shoots]
> *Tony, see if you can dispose of that."*
>
> – HANS GRUBER

It's true.
I wasn't at my best anymore,
and that night outside stage door
after *Coppelia*, he told me straight:

At twenty-eight your dancing

has waned, these teenagers
have stolen the stage – you did once,
no mistake – but wouldn't you

try a new turn,

your upper-body strength could be
used in my firm and the force
of your fouetté *would keep even*

the most vicious assailant at bay.
Now,

that isn't to say you'd be attacked…
it's more a glissade *or two*
in a pre-planned move...

… it's our style, you see,

we're looking to improve.
He put a hand to my gut:
Tell me there's not

    a movement in here

when you think: chassé
from behind a building strut,
an HK94 to cover men

    running to the doors?
        And if the guards

decide to fire back, how about some of those
grand sissonne *or* pas de chats
that we saw tonight?

    He leaned into my ear:

My boy, you'd be out of sight. And I was,
until I leapt on that forthright cop
who spun and flung me throttled,

    broken-necked, on steps

between two skyscraper floors. But, Hans,
I knew my swansong – that off-hand
pas de deux – must've been something

    fit to die for.

MIKEY TANDINO

        can talk about himself
in the third person as his god-given
Italian-American action movie right.
Mikey can brag and incite crime, insist
he's done his time and gone straight –
unless, that is, fate finds him
in Beverly Hills working security,
enough bearer bonds up for grabs
to make pure this or any city.

        Axel, come back with me to Rodeo Drive,
        let's steal a car, ditch your rust bucket
        and Detroit, and bust shifts down 80, 70, 15.

Cut clean from this cop shit, man.
We'd make a killing out West
in drugs or hits, they've oil to dig for
or else two hoodlum kids like us
could have success on screen – sign up
with William Morris and they'll be chiselling
our names before the 80s are out. Head
south with me brother where my nous
and your mouth can get us into trouble.

        I tell you, down there the streets are lined
        with palms, paved with money and –
        you have to believe me – it's sunny
        all year round.

GARLAND GREENE

Admit it, you like me, and the muzzle
and chains only put you off slightly
because before I arrived on this plane you'd only known
knuckleheads conforming to clichés
or Hollywood heroes doing the same, and fortune
smiles on the thoughtful, the measurably sane.

So, when they were refueling and I chose not
to make a thirty-fourth victim of the local girl, sang her
hymns instead, you warmed to my part: recognised
my arc on its upward loop and found yourself
rooting for me over Virus and Baby-O
and the others whose mothers held them

too much or not enough. Then my somehow
contriving to slip from the plane crash
unscathed in Vegas – the wreckage roughing up
the Strip – brought you to your feet;
and while the usual showdown stormed
through terrified streets, you were

thinking of me. And I you of course.
We're all unlikely stars, or maybe playing
the right parts in the wrong movies, aren't we?
Perhaps we'll meet in our own sequels, cross paths
on empty desert roads on my way South, or share
exophthalmic glances in a Tijuana bar

that I'll learn to call my sweet home.
Life, as you know, is just a series of rolls, and all
we can hope is we're standing near the edge
of the table with the dice in our hands
when the croupier asks: *Does the new shooter
feel lucky? Well, does he?*

HELEN

Pop Quiz, Sam: There's a lady two seats back,
advancing in years but devoted and true,
with a view out the windshield to Tarmac
futures alongside you. What do you do?

Perhaps this metaphor's confused. I'll be blunt.
Remember the one scared of the freeway
and being confined; who sits at the front
of your bus, doe-eyed every weekday;

who waits in the morning till three have passed by
for your silver carriage; who cradled your chest
when that bullet ripped in; who heard you'd die
in your whisper and who followed you, pressed

into the road? I'm Helen. I hope they'll write about us,
Sam, and our too-short time on this too-fast bus.

NOTES

Lloyd owns a truck stop diner on a back route to North Los Angeles. (*Terminator 2: Judgment Day*, 1991)

Hawkins is the youngest member of Major Alan "Dutch" Schaefer's elite team, sent into a Central American jungle to rescue a cabinet minister abducted by guerrilla forces. (*Predator*, 1987)

Benny, a cop, is killed in a tearoom shoot-out with an arms gang. His best friend, Tequila, is bent on revenge. (*Hard Boiled*, 1992)

Timmy, the young son of the Jorden family – part of a team terraforming the planet Acheron – witnesses, alongside his younger sister Newt, a facehugger impregnate his father with a chestburster. (*Aliens*, 1986)

Admiral Chuck Farrell, Royal Canadian Navy, is the highest-ranking officer due to be present at a Tiger Helicopter secret demonstration, before he is seduced by the assassin Xenia Onatopp. (*Goldeneye*, 1995)

Donald Gennaro, a lawyer representing investors, accompanies the endorsement team to inspect Jurassic Park's viability and security. (*Jurassic Park*, 1993)

Cougar, the number one pilot in flight school, goes into shock as an enemy plane trains a missile on him. Pete "Maverick" Mitchell guides him back to base and Cougar "turns in his wings". (*Top Gun*, 1986)

GIRL, who we find out later to be Amanda Hunsaker, throws herself from a residential tower block prompting a criminal investigation into a drugs ring. (*Lethal Weapon*, 1987)

Tony is a member of Hans Gruber's team infiltrating the Nakatomi Plaza Building during a Christmas party. (*Die Hard*, 1988)

Mikey Tandino is an old school friend of Detroit policeman Axel Foley. In and out of trouble with the law, Mikey pays with his life for having left California with bearer bonds stolen from an organised crime outfit. (*Beverly Hills Cop*, 1984)

Garland Greene, otherwise known as "The Marietta Mangler", killed over 30 people before being captured. He was being moved between institutions on a flight hijacked by prisoners. (*Con Air*, 1997)

Helen catches the 2525 bus running downtown from Venice every morning. (*Speed*, 1994)

ACKNOWLEDGEMENTS

Thanks to Lizzie Green, my family and friends for their unending support and enthusiasm; to Billy Pitchford, John-Paul Pierrot, David Isaac and David McDonagh for their advice and encouragement; to Kayo Chingonyi, Tracy Horn, Anna Kirk, Rachel Piercey, Lyn Thornton and Emma Wright for their invaluable feedback; to Helen Farish, Andrew Motion, Jo Shapcott; to the editors of *Aspidistra*, *Bedford Square 5* and *Inky Needles* where some of these poems have been published; and to Arnie, Bruce, Keanu, Sly, Tom and the others.

ABOUT THE POET

James Trevelyan grew up in the Midlands and now lives in London. His poems have been published in print and online magazines, and anthologised by the Emma Press. He is Poetry Reviews Editor for *The Cadaverine* magazine and works for the independent publisher Penned in the Margins.

ABOUT THE ILLUSTRATOR

Emma Wright studied Classics at Brasenose College, Oxford. She worked in ebook production at Orion Publishing Group before leaving to set up the Emma Press in 2012. In 2015 she was awarded a grant from Arts Council England to run a poetry tour for children. She lives in Birmingham.

The Emma Press

small press, big dreams

The Emma Press is an independent publisher dedicated to producing beautiful, thought-provoking books. It was founded in 2012 by Emma Wright in Winnersh, UK, and is now based in Birmingham. The Emma Press was shortlisted for the Michael Marks Award for Poetry Pamphlet Publishers in both 2014 and 2015.

In July-November 2015 we travelled around the country with 'Myths and Monsters', a poetry tour aimed at children aged 8+. This was made possible with a grant from Grants for the Arts, supported using public funding by the National Lottery through Arts Council England.

Our publishing programme features a mixture of themed poetry anthologies and single-author pamphlets, with an ongoing engagement with the works of the Roman poet Ovid. We publish books which excite us and are often on the lookout for new writing.

Sign up to the monthly Emma Press newsletter to hear about our events, publications and upcoming calls for submissions. Our books are available to buy from our online shop, as well as to order or buy from bookshops.

http://theemmapress.com
http://emmavalleypress.blogspot.co.uk/